The Journey of Lewis and Clark

EXPLORATION AND DISCOVERY

EXPLORATION
AND DISCOVERY

The Journey of Lewis and Clark

How the Corps of Discovery explored
the Louisiana Purchase, reached the
Pacific Ocean, and returned safely

Rob Staeger

Mason Crest Publishers
Philadelphia

This book is dedicated to Will Eisner,
a pioneer of the imagination.

Produced by OTTN Publishing, Stockton, N.J.

Mason Crest Publishers
370 Reed Road
Broomall PA 19008

Mason Crest Publishers' world wide web address is
www.masoncrest.com

3 5 7 9 8 6 4 2

Library of Congress Cataloging-in-Publication Data

Staeger, Rob.
  The journey of Lewis and Clark: how the Corps of Discovery
explored the Louisiana Purchase, reached the Pacific Ocean, and
returned safely / Rob Staeger.
    p. cm. — (Exploration and discovery)
Summary: Discusses the 1804-1806 Lewis and Clark expedition, or Corps of
Discovery, which explored the vast region acquired by the United States in
the Louisiana Purchase seeking the Northwest Passage to the Pacific.
  Includes bibliographical references
  ISBN 1-59084-056-9
1. Lewis and Clark Expedition (1804-1806)—Juvenile literature. 2. West
(U.S.)—Discovery and exploration—Juvenile literature. 3. West (U.S.)—
Description and travel—Juvenile literature. [1. Lewis and Clark Expedition
(1804-1806) 2. West (U.S.)—Discovery and exploration.]
I. Title. II. Exploration and discovery (Philadelphia, Pa.)
F592.7 .S685 2003
917.804'2—dc21
                                                          2002009152

EXPLORATION AND DISCOVERY

Contents

This statue of Meriwether Lewis and William Clark, titled "Explorers at the Portage," overlooks the spot where the Missouri and Sun Rivers converge in Montana. Between 1804 and 1806, Lewis and Clark led a group of explorers from St. Louis across the unmapped wilderness of North America to the Pacific Ocean.

The Vote

LEWIS AND Clark brought many things home from their historic journey across North America in the early years of the 19th century. They had skins of elk, antelope, and buffalo. They brought Osage oranges and clippings of evergreen huckleberry. At one point, they even sent back a live prairie dog and four live magpies.

They also gave gifts to the Indian tribes they met along their route. They gave special medals, symbolizing friendship with the United States. They gave out scissors and knives, razors and thimbles. They bargained with whiskey and tobacco. They even gave one tribe a mechanical corn grinder. There was one thing, however, that they kept with them all the way to the west coast—democracy.

In November 1805, the expedition was faced with a choice. They needed to build a winter fort. They could build it on the north side of the Columbia River, among the Chinook Indians, or they could build it on the south shore, with a tribe of Clatsop Indians. Either place would give them a chance to catch a merchant ship home. However, the coastal area was wet, and bound to be icy during winter. Their third choice was to retrace their steps. They could build a fort miles inland, where it was much drier, but they would never know if a ship had arrived.

This was an important decision, one that could determine whether their mission was successful or not. Their lives may have depended on it. The captains decided to take a vote.

They were under no obligation to do so. Even though they were standing in what would one day be Washington State, they were no longer in America. They were in the Oregon Territory. While the expedition was not a war party, it was a military unit. Lewis and Clark were the commanders and were entitled to give orders. They both felt that the south shore of the river was the best place to stay. However, the captains felt even more strongly that the decision belonged in the hands of the entire company.

The vote was remarkable for another reason as well.

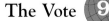

Naturally, Lewis and Clark voted, as did every man in the military unit. However, the civilians on the trip were given the opportunity to vote as well, including the party's translators, George Drouillard and Toussaint Charbonneau; Charbonneau's Native American wife, Sacagawea; and Clark's African-American slave, York. Women were almost a century away from getting the vote. Native Americans were not considered citizens. Most black men, including York, had no rights at all.

In the end, the vote was almost **unanimous**. Except for one man, everyone voted to stay on the south shore, just as Lewis and Clark had originally suggested.

Despite the difficulties that Lewis and Clark had encountered on their long journey west, the two leaders of the Corps of Discovery were committed to American principles of freedom and democracy. Their historic journey between 1804 and 1806 would open the American West to eventual settlement, and help the United States one day stretch from the Atlantic Ocean to the Pacific.

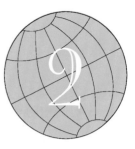

Thomas Jefferson was president of the United States in 1803, when the French emperor Napoleon offered to sell the United States the vast Louisiana Territory. Jefferson had already planned to send a group of Americans to find out what the unmapped land held. After the deal was done, the party's mission was to determine exactly what Jefferson had purchased.

Instructions and Preparations

PRESIDENT THOMAS Jefferson was a curious man. When he took office in 1801, the United States stretched from the east coast to the Mississippi River. Beyond the river was a vast, unexplored country.

Jefferson was curious to know what lay beyond the Mississippi. The Lewis and Clark expedition was born out of this curiosity. He wanted to send a group of men west to find out. However, Congress would have to pay for it. To get money from Congress, Jefferson wrote, "We can steal the fur trade from the British. And it would not cost much, only $2,500." Jefferson knew that curiosity alone would not be enough to get Congress to agree. But by combining business with a jab at the British, Jefferson knew he had a winning combination.

American and British ships traded for furs with Indians on the west coast. To get there, they had to sail around Cape Horn, the southern tip of South America. Many people believed that a water route stretched across the continent, called the **northwest passage**. If this passage were found, the fur trade would be less expensive for Americans. This would give them an advantage.

The expedition was to be called the Corps of Discovery. Jefferson asked his 28-year-old assistant, Meriwether Lewis, to lead it. Jefferson knew Lewis had a sharp mind, military experience, and an interest in the west. Lewis excitedly took on the challenge.

Lewis was to follow the Missouri River to its source. He would then map the river and the land between it and a westward-flowing river. While doing this, Lewis needed to keep a careful journal. Jefferson stressed this point in his instructions to Lewis. "Your observations are to be taken with great pains & accuracy, to be entered distinctly, & intelligibly for others as well as yourself."

Lewis's notes would be important keys to unlocking the west. For safety, he would make several copies of his journals. Jefferson even suggested making a copy on sturdy birch paper, which was harder to destroy. Lewis was to note

President Jefferson carefully prepared Meriwether Lewis to lead the Corps of Discovery, as the group making the westward expedition became known. Lewis received training in medicine, astronomy, botany, and mapmaking.

everything in his journal, including geography, climate, and minerals. He would describe any plants and animals he saw. New species were particularly important.

Jefferson was particularly curious about the Indian nations. He wanted to know who they were and what lands they controlled. He wanted to know how the tribes got along. He was interested in their clothing, food, tools, and laws. Most of all, he wanted to know how to trade with the Native American tribes.

Jefferson wanted the Indians treated with respect and friendship. Lewis could invite chiefs to meet with the president. Some native children could even be educated in U.S. schools. It was all part of the strategy to open *trade relations* with Indians.

Jefferson warned Lewis not to take foolish risks. He knew the expedition might encounter hostility. The group could fight off small attacks, but if Lewis ever thought that they would not survive a battle, Jefferson wanted him to return home rather than risk losing the information gathered by the expedition.

After traveling to the west coast by land, the expedition could return by sea. A merchant ship on the coast would take the men home, or at least a pair of men with the journals. Jefferson wrote Lewis a letter of credit, promising that the government would pay for their return trip.

Lewis spent April in Philadelphia preparing for the trip. He learned all he could about medicine from Doctor Benjamin Rush, America's most famous doctor at the time.

When he was planning his expedition, Lewis asked William Clark to share the leadership of the Corps of Discovery. Lewis had served under Clark in the U.S. Army several years before.

Lewis also learned how to preserve plant and animal specimens and made *celestial* observations. The alignment of stars and planets could tell Lewis where he was.

In Philadelphia, Lewis bought the expedition's gear. Overall, he spent almost $2,500 to outfit the party. The most expensive thing he bought was a *chronometer*, for $250. The stars could tell Lewis his *latitude*, but he needed an accurate timepiece to know his *longitude*. Lewis also bought medicine, axes, fishing hooks and line, woolen overalls, and plenty of paper, pencils, and rifle powder. He was issued 30 Kentucky rifles, the best rifles the army had.

Lewis also bought gifts for the Indian tribes he would meet. These were small, useful

One of the strangest items that Lewis and Clark took with them on their expedition was an experimental air rifle. Lewis may have brought the weapon hoping to conserve gunpowder. The gun used compressed air, which was forced by a hand pump into a round metal chamber. When the chamber was filled with air, the gun could fire about 15 shots. As it turned out, the .28 caliber bullet that the air gun fired was not large enough to kill wild game that the party could eat. However, the gun did impress Native Americans the party met along the way to the Pacific. These Indians believed that a rifle that could be fired without gunpower was magical.

This is the remains of one of the peace medals which the Corps of Discovery took with them on their journey. The reverse side contained an image of President Jefferson.

items, such as thimbles, razors, and scissors. He also brought "peace medals." These were large metal coins with a picture of President Jefferson on one side and a picture of two hands shaking on the other. Lewis gave these to the chiefs of every tribe they met.

In June, Lewis told Jefferson that he wanted to share command of the expedition. The person he had in mind was William Clark. Lewis had served under Clark in the army, and he and Lewis were still close friends.

Lewis wrote to Clark, offering to share command with him. He promised that the War Department would make Clark a captain. Lewis con-

Lewis designed the lead canisters that held the expedition's gunpowder. When melted down, they made the right number of lead balls for the amount of powder they held.

cluded, "If there is anything in this enterprise which would induce you to participate in its fatiegues [sic], its dangers and its honors, believe me there is no man on

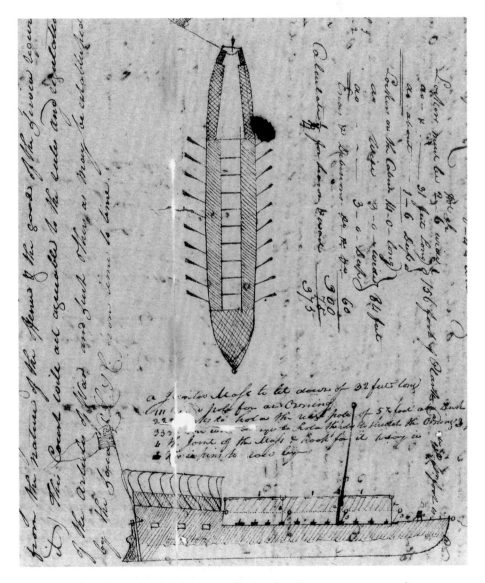

Lewis ordered a special boat, called a keelboat, to carry the party up the Missouri River. This page from Lewis's journal shows drawings of the boat.

earth with whom I should feel equal pleasure in sharing them with as yourself."

Clark quickly accepted. He assured Lewis that, "no man lives whith whome I would perfur to undertake Such a Trip." Thus, one of the greatest partnerships in history had begun.

In fact, Lewis wasn't able to keep one of his promises. The War Department refused to make Clark a captain. They made him a lieutenant instead. Lewis decided, however, that there was no reason to tell their men that. Throughout the expedition, they called each other "Captain Lewis" and "Captain Clark." None of their men knew the truth.

Aside from two capable leaders, the expedition had one more thing in its favor. On July 4, 1803, the Louisiana Purchase was announced. For $15 million, the United States had bought 820,000 square miles of land west of the Mississippi River. This meant that the expedition would be traveling through U.S. territory all the way to the Rocky Mountains. It was now much less likely that other countries would interfere. Suddenly, Lewis and Clark's mission had become more important. They would be the first explorers in America's new land.

Lewis designed a boat for the expedition. It was a 55-foot-long **keelboat**. It held 22 men and 12 tons of weight. It

Treaty

Between the United States of America

and the French Republic

The President of the United States of America and the First Consul of the French Republic in the name of the French People desiring to remove all Sources of misunderstanding relative to objects of discussion mentioned in the Second and fifth articles of the Convention of the {8th Vendémiaire an 9 / 30 September 1800} relative to the rights claimed by the United States in virtue of the Treaty concluded at Madrid the 27 of October 1795 between His Catholic Majesty, & the Said United States, & willing to Strengthen the union and friendship which at the time of the Said Convention was happily reestablished between the two nations have respectively named their Plenipotentiaries to wit The President of the United States, by and with the advice and consent of the Senate of the Said State; Robert R. Livingston Minister Plenipotentiary of the United State and James Monroe Minister Plenipotentiary and Envoy extraordinary of the Said State near the Government of the French Republic; And the First Consul in the name of the French people, Citizen Francis Barbé Marbois Minister of the public treasury who after having respectively exchanged their full powers have agreed to the following

articles

The first page of the treaty that gave the United States the Louisiana Territory in for $15 million—less than 3 cents an acre.

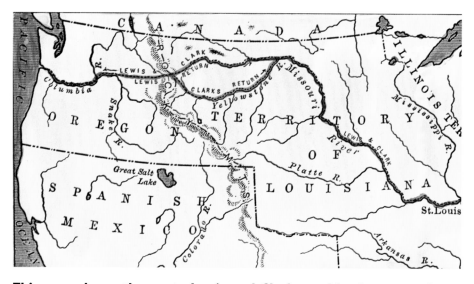

This map shows the route Lewis and Clark would take to reach the Pacific Ocean. At the time Spain still controlled much of the American southwest as well as Mexico. The United States had purchased the 820,000 square miles of the Louisiana Territory from France for $15 million. Ownership of the Oregon Territory, which includes the present-day states of Washington and Oregon, was uncertain. Both the United States and Great Britain claimed the land. The present-day border with Canada, which is shown on this map, would not be established for another 40 years.

was built in Pittsburgh, and took six weeks longer than expected to complete. Impatient, Lewis visited the shipyard every day. Eventually, he bought a Newfoundland dog to take his mind off the boat. The dog's name was Seaman.

Clark hired men for the mission. He looked for young, unmarried men with useful skills. He needed carpenters, blacksmiths, hunters, and boatmen. There were hundreds of volunteers to choose from. Clark picked a dozen men—two sergeants and 10 privates.

The expedition would begin in St. Louis, the center of the fur trade. After rowing the keelboat to St. Louis, the captains realized they needed more muscle power. Clark recruited another dozen soldiers to help. They spent the winter outside St. Louis. By the time they left, the Corps of Discovery consisted of 34 men. Among the military were 22 privates, three sergeants, and Lewis and Clark themselves. Four civilians served with them. Three of them were interpreters. One was named George Drouillard. Drouillard was a skilled woodsman and knew several Indian languages. They paid him $25 a month for his services.

The fourth civilian was York, Clark's African-American slave. York was a strong, agile man who had served Clark since they were children. Because he was a slave, he was paid nothing.

Five more soldiers came with the expedition. After the first winter, they would return to St. Louis, bringing news, plant and animal specimens, and copies of the commanders' journals. On May 21, 1804, the Corps of Discovery officially began its journey west.

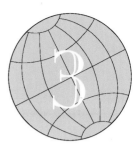

During the 1830s, an artist named George Catlin became famous for his western scenes. He painted many of the places Lewis and Clark had visited on their journey 30 years earlier, including this view of the Mandan Indian village where they spent the winter of 1804–05.

Up the Missouri to the Mandan

THE EXPEDITION left St. Louis in three boats—two smaller boats, called pirogues, and Lewis' keelboat. Soldiers also led two horses along the Missouri's banks.

Progress was difficult. The river's current pushed against them constantly. Every so often, the wind was right and they raised the sails. Usually, however, they had to row. They steered the ship from *eddy* to eddy, trying to keep clear of the main current. *Snags*, collapsing riverbanks, and sudden storms slowed the group down. Storms ended as quickly as they began. In some places, the men had to leave the boat. They hauled it forward with ropes and brute strength. This is called cordelling.

Clark kept track of their progress using a process called *dead reckoning*. Eyeing a landmark up the river, he would estimate the distance to it. Once he reached it, he would mark the distance down. Then he would find another landmark and repeat the process. In this way, Clark mapped the river. There was a great deal of room for error in the process. A person needed excellent judgment to do it well.

Clark usually stayed on the boat. Lewis often rode one of the horses, jotting notes about the plants and animals he saw. At one point, he and a few men went to investigate some Native American etchings on a rock. He wrote, "We had not landed 3 Minites before three verry large Snakes was observed in the Crevises of the rocks & killed." Danger, it appeared, could be hiding anywhere.

The Great Plains was a startling sight to the captains. They were both Virginians, used to hills and forests. Here, there were no trees. Herds of deer and buffalo spread across the prairie. Lewis estimated one herd of buffalo at 3,000.

Every day brought some new wonder. The group found coyotes, jackrabbits, and antelope. They also discovered prairie dogs. They called these "barking squirrels" in the journals. They spent a day trying to flood prairie dogs out of their holes, hoping to capture a live one. They finally succeeded. Months later, they sent it back to President Jefferson.

Meriwether Lewis

Meriwether Lewis was born in Virginia in 1774. His father was Lieutenant William Lewis, an officer who served in the Continental Army during the American Revolution. Meriwether's mother, Lucy Meriwether Lewis Marks, was an expert in herbal remedies. Meriwether demonstrated a curiosity about nature at an early age. He was also an excellent hunter.

Lewis served in the Pennsylvania militia in 1794 and fought in the Whiskey Rebellion. Soon afterward, he transferred to the regular army. There, he served six months under William Clark.

When Thomas Jefferson became president in 1801, he made Lewis his personal secretary. The men had long conversations about science, politics, and the west. In 1803, Jefferson asked Lewis to head an expedition up the Missouri River to the Pacific Ocean. Lewis asked his trusted friend William Clark to share the command, who accepted. Lewis and Clark left St. Louis in 1804 with nearly three dozen men. By the winter of 1805, they had reached the Pacific Ocean.

When they returned, Lewis was given 1,600 acres of land as a reward. He became governor of the Louisiana Territory in 1808. Jefferson urged Lewis to publish a book about the expedition, but Lewis couldn't bring himself to write it.

In 1809, Lewis was traveling to Washington, D.C., when he checked into an inn and shot himself.

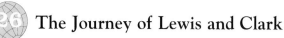

On the evening of August 2, a group of Otos and Missouri Indians entered the expedition's campsite. These were the first Indians the group met. The next day, Lewis delivered a speech to them, addressing the Indians as "Children" of the "Great Father," President Jefferson. He told them the French and Spanish had left the area, leaving it to "the Seventeen Great Nations of America."

He offered the United States' protection and the hope of trade. When he finished, Lewis gave gifts and a peace medal to every tribe. The gifts weren't much, but Lewis' speech was well received. An Oto chief asked for some gunpowder and whiskey, which Lewis gave to him.

Near the end of August, one of the sergeants became quite ill. Most likely, Sergeant Charles Floyd had a burst appendix. He died on August 20. The expedition buried him on a round hill near present-day Sioux City, Iowa, and named it Floyd's Bluff.

Further up the river, the group encountered the Teton Sioux, or Lakota. They were a powerful tribe, and Lewis and Clark had been told they would not be friendly. They stopped travelers on the river, bullying people into paying a *toll*. Most travelers gave in.

The captains showed some of the Lakota chiefs around their boat. Everyone drank some whiskey. One of the chiefs pretended to be drunk, bumping into things and trying to cause trouble. On their way back to shore, one of the Lakota grabbed a rope on the pirogue. He said they hadn't been given enough valuable presents and he wanted the boat.

Lakota warriors lined the shore, but Clark refused to be bullied. He drew his sword. Soon, the keelboat pulled around. The men of the expedition aimed their guns at the Lakota. It was a standoff.

Eventually, Clark pulled the boat away from the shore, and the dispute was settled peacefully. Clark's bravery

George Catlin painted this view of Floyd's Bluff, the hill where Lewis and Clark buried Sergeant Charles Floyd. Amazingly, Floyd was the only man who died during the expedition.

against the Lakota helped them later, as well. Another tribe, the Arikara, was generally hostile to whites. But when the Corps of Discovery entered their territory, they were friendly. They had already heard that bullying would get them nowhere.

By October, the expedition reached a Mandan village. This was the furthest outpost for trappers. At the time the Mandan village was very large. More people lived there than in Washington, D.C. The expedition planned to spend their winter there. Beyond the Mandan village was unknown territory.

Lewis and Clark gave a metal corn grinder to the Mandan nation. Such a large gift set the tone for their relations throughout the winter. The Mandan invited them to build a fort across the river from the village. The American explorers were living in the unfinished Fort Mandan by the end of November, and had finished the fort by Christmas.

Clark's slave, York, puzzled the Mandans. They had never seen a black man before. They thought he might be an animal or a spirit. For a while, York pretended to be a bear to frighten Mandan children. Apparently, he was too scary, because Clark made him stop.

> **In covering the 4,000 miles they traveled between St. Louis and the west coast, Clark's estimations were off by only 40 miles.**

In late November, a Mandan man was killed in a fight with the Sioux. Clark wasted no time in gathering most of the men and offering their help. Things were settled without bloodshed, but Clark's willingness to help showed the Mandan that they were trusted *allies*.

During the winter, the Mandan brought the group food. In exchange, members of the Corps repaired some of the Mandan's tools and kettles. Lewis became the village doctor. On February 7, he helped the wife of a fur trapper give birth to a baby boy. The trapper's name was Toussaint Charbonneau. His wife's name was Sacagawea. The captains hired Charbonneau as an interpreter, knowing that Sacagawea would come along. She, they guessed, would be an excellent guide to the area. They were right. During the trip Sacagawea proved herself extremely valuable to the party.

On April 7, 1805, the expedition left the village. Sacagawea carried her son, Jean-Baptiste, on her back. From now on, they had no map. They were sailing up the Missouri into the unknown.

The Corps of Discovery met many Native American tribes during their adventures in the northwest. Most were friendly but curious. Because the party included a woman and child, the Indians understood that Lewis and Clark's intentions were peaceful.

The Mandan to the Rockies

THE MANDAN gave Lewis and Clark a description of the land they were heading into. They would reach a waterfall, the Mandan said. After that, the river would take them into the mountains. The captains expected a fairly quick journey to the coast. They thought it would take half a day to get around the waterfall, and expected to cross the mountains in a few days. They thought they could make it to the coast and back to the Mandan village by winter. They had no idea what they were up against.

Before they left, the captains sent a boat back down the Missouri River. It carried copies of their journals, maps, plant clippings, animal skins, and even the live prairie dog.

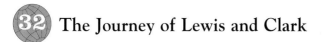

Of the new members, Sacagawea was usually more helpful than her husband. At one point, Charbonneau lost control of his boat, and it was Sacagawea who kept it from capsizing. Throughout the trip, she kept Jean-Baptiste in a

Sacagawea, standing with Lewis and Clark, points the way in this painting. The Shoshone woman would prove to be a great help to

cradleboard on her back. Clark liked the boy and nick-
named him "Little Pomp."

The group continued to find new creatures. The grizzly
bear was the most ferocious. At first, Lewis thought their

**the Corps of Discovery, even though she carried her infant son in a
basket on her back for most of the journey.**

rifles would keep them safe. A few days later, however, he had changed his mind. He had seen a grizzly get shot 10 times and continue to live for 20 minutes. Soon, no one hunted without a partner.

By the end of May, the company saw mountains in the distance. The waterfall couldn't be too far away, they thought. But a few days later, the mountains seemed no closer. Even worse, the expedition had come to a fork in the river. One fork was the Missouri. The other was a smaller river that fed into it. However, they couldn't tell which was which. The northern fork was deeper than the southern one. The current was slower. Its water was a muddy brown, like the Missouri's. Most of the men thought this was the Missouri River.

Lewis and Clark disagreed. The southern fork was clear and fast. The stones on the river bottom were round and flat. That was common to many rivers that began in the mountains.

Wasting time traveling up the wrong river could cost the expedition several weeks, so the captains split up. They each led a small, quick group up the forks. Lewis took the south fork, and Clark took the north. After a few days, both captains turned back. They were certain the southern fork was the Missouri.

When both captains had rejoined the main group, they

William Clark

William Clark was born in Virginia in 1770. His older brother, George Rogers Clark, was a famous Revolutionary War general. William joined the army in 1789 and fought in several battles against the Native Americans.

While in the army, Clark commanded a sharp-shooter unit. Meriwether Lewis was part of that squad. They served together for six months. It was the start of a lifelong friendship.

Clark left the army in 1796 and spent the next seven years on the frontier. In 1803, Lewis invited him to share command of the Corps of Discovery, and Clark jumped at the chance. He was strong and healthy, and his skills complemented Lewis perfectly. Clark was better at commanding enlisted men and a better sailor. Plus, he was an excellent mapmaker.

The expedition took over two years. When Clark returned, President Jefferson made him Superintendent of Indian Affairs. Clark was concerned about Native Americans, often fighting for justice on their behalf. He served at the post for 30 years. Clark was also the governor of the Missouri Territory from 1813 to 1821.

Clark married Julia Hancock in 1808. Their first of five sons was born in 1809. Clark named him Meriwether Lewis Clark. Clark lived to be 68. In September of 1838, he died after a short illness.

announced they would take the south fork. Lewis paddled ahead to find the waterfall. He reached it on June 13. Lewis called it "the grandest sight I ever beheld." The falls were amazing. The waterfall in front of him was a 40-foot drop. Upriver was another drop of 19 feet. Beyond that were three more falls. The captains had expected a half-day *portage* around one waterfall. Instead, they had to avoid 12 miles of dangerous river.

Clark took charge of the portage, plotting a trail for the crew to follow. It would take them 17 miles over harsh land. The expedition built frames out of cottonwood to help carry

As they traveled, Lewis and Clark each kept careful diaries. Much of what we know about the adventures of the Corps of Discovery is contained in these logs. Clark would later edit the diaries for publication. The page above, in Clark's handwriting, features a drawing of an evergreen shrub. The diaries were wrapped in leather (opposite) to protect them from foul weather.

their equipment. It would be a long, difficult walk.

The portage took its toll on the expedition. The trail was covered in cactus. Needles constantly pricked their hands and feet. The barbs shredded moccasins after only two days. Mosquitoes were everywhere. Days were either too hot, or cold and wet. Sometimes the group was hit with fist-sized hail. Sometimes the high winds helped. Men carrying boats raised the sail, and the wind lightened their load until it changed direction.

In the end, it took a full month to get around the Great Falls. On July 15, they were back on the Missouri. The party carved two more **dugouts** to replace a large **bullboat**. The Missouri River turned south after the Great Falls. On July 25, the party came to a three-way fork. Lewis and Clark named one tributary the Jefferson River. The other two tributaries were named for James Madison, who was

President Jefferson's secretary of state, and Albert Gallatin, the secretary of the treasury.

The Corps of Discovery followed the fork Lewis and Clark had named the Jefferson. Sacagawea recognized a few landmarks. In the distance, she saw where her people, the Shoshone, had crossed the Bitterroot Mountains.

Lewis, George Drouillard, John Shields, and Hugh McNeal scouted ahead, following the river up the mountains. On their way, they saw a Shoshone man. It was important to meet with the Shoshones. The expedition needed to trade with them to get horses. They wouldn't make it to the Columbia River without them.

The Shoshone man stood about 100 yards away. Lewis shouted, "Ta-ba-bone!" Sacagawea had told him it was the Shoshone word for "friend." The man saw Lewis approach and ran away. No one was close enough to catch him.

Today there is a bronze marker at the three forks of the Missouri River. Lewis and Clark reached the forks at the end of July, and followed one branch of the river into the Bitterroot Mountains.

Eventually, the Missouri became a small creek trickling down from the mountains. Hugh McNeal put one foot on either side of it. He "thanked his god that he had lived to bestride the mighty & heretofore deemed endless Missouri," Lewis wrote. They had found the source of the Missouri River at last.

> **"Ta-ba-bone" did not actually mean "friend" in Shoshone. Due to a translation mix-up, Sacagawea had told Lewis the word for "stranger." No wonder the Shoshone man ran away!**

After drinking from the ice-cold water, the group climbed a ridge. Lewis expected to see the Columbia River below them. He got quite a shock. Instead of the river, he saw miles of mountains. He had never seen a mountain range spread so far. No river would take them through it. Without horses, they would either have to turn back or die.

A group of Indians watches from a bluff over the Columbia River as Lewis and Clark's party makes progress west.

To the Pacific

THE NEXT day, Lewis spotted three more Shoshone. There was an old woman, a teenager, and a young child. The teen ran off, but the woman and child didn't move. Soon, several Shoshone warriors arrived at the site. Lewis told them "Ta-ba-bone" and put down his gun. Droillard's sign language convinced the warriors to take them to their village. Lewis told them about the rest of his group. He said they had a Shoshone woman with them. He also mentioned York. The Shoshone were eager to meet the black man.

Lewis convinced the Shoshone to come to a camp along Beaverhead Creek, where he expected to find the rest of the Corps. The place was empty. Some of the warriors thought

41

it was a trap. To prove it was safe, Lewis borrowed one of their cloaks. If it was a trap, the cloak would make him a target.

On the morning of August 17, Lewis spotted Clark, Charbonneau, and Sacagawea. Soon, the group was speaking with the chief, named Cameahwait. The translation was complicated. Lewis or Clark would speak in English. Then Charbonneau would tell Sacagawea what they wanted in Hidatsa. Next, Sacagawea would speak Shoshone to Cameahwait. When Cameahwait responded, the process reversed itself.

In the middle of this, Sacagawea sprang up and hugged the chief. She had suddenly recognized Cameahwait. He was her brother.

From then on, the talks went smoothly. The Shoshone knew a way to cross the Rocky Mountains. The Nez Perce used it every year. They had a guide named Old Toby who would take them across.

Because of Sacagawea, Lewis and Clark were able to get horses cheaply. Eventually, they bought 29 horses to take their goods across the mountains.

On September 1, the expedition started toward the Bitterroot Mountains. Looking up at the Bitterroots, Sergeant Gass called them "the most terrible mountains I ever beheld." The sight of the Bitterroots, however, was

The Shoshone meet Lewis and Clark, who are at the right in this painting. During their meeting in the Lemhi River Valley, Sacagawea was reunited with her brother, Cameahwait. The Shoshone agreed to help the Corps of Discovery cross the western mountains.

nothing compared to crossing them. There was hardly anything to eat on the mountains. Hunting groups regularly returned empty-handed. The men killed one of their colts for food. The group was pelted by snow, hail, and freezing rain. To make matters worse, Old Toby lost track of the trail. No one had any idea when they would get across the mountains. They were staying alive, but barely.

Clark scouted ahead of the party. On September 19, he found a stray horse, killed it, and ate some with his group. He hung the meat on a tree for the rest of the expedition. On September 20, Clark's party finally made it out of the mountains. Some Nez Perce Indians met him. Clark spoke with Twisted Hair, their chief. The captain and his men spent the night in the Nez Perce teepees. Two days later, Lewis' group joined them. Weak from their experience in the mountains, they became extremely ill.

The Nez Perce decided to kill the newcomers while they were still weak and sick. Their valuables would make the Nez Perce the most powerful tribe in the region overnight.

One woman changed their minds. Her name was Watkuweis, which meant "Returned from a Far Country." She had been kidnapped by Blackfeet Indians years before and sold to a white trader in Canada, who had treated her well. Since a white man had helped Watkuweis, she helped the white men in return. Her words spared their lives.

In a week, the party was ready to move on. They had made it to the Columbia River by October 6. They dug out several new canoes and pushed off that afternoon. For the first time, the current helped them. They floated downriver at seven miles per hour. Compared to their trip up the Missouri, this was a blistering pace.

The group made excellent progress. Twisted Hair and some other chiefs rode ahead of them, telling people to treat the group well. Across the mountains, there were no more buffalo to hunt. Instead, salmon leapt across the surface of the Columbia. The men did not like to eat salmon. Instead,

Sacagawea

Sacagawea was born in a Shoshone village in either western Montana or eastern Idaho. Around 1800, a Hidatsa raiding party kidnapped her. The Hidatsa probably gave her the name "Sacagawea," which means "Bird Woman."

In 1804, Sacagawea was sold to a French trapper named Toussaint Charbonneau, who married her. They settled in a Mandan village along the Missouri River.

The village also served as a winter camp for the Lewis and Clark expedition. Lewis and Clark hired Charbonneau as an interpreter, and Sacagawea came with him. Sacagawea was a great help to the explorers. She found many fruits and vegetables, which rounded out their diets. Later, the group found the Shoshone Indians. The chief was her brother. This made trading with the Shoshone much easier.

Sacagawea traveled to St. Louis in 1809, bringing her son for Captain Clark to educate. Sacagawea probably died a few years later in South Dakota. Some people believe that she rejoined the Shoshone, however, and lived until 1884.

In 2000, Sacagawea was honored by the United States. Her image is on a new one-dollar coin.

they bargained with the local tribes for dogs to eat. Lewis enjoyed the dog meat, but Clark never got used to it.

Soon after they reached the Snake River, the river churned into rapids. In one short stretch, the river dropped 38 feet. To be safe, they should have carried their canoes around the rapids. Instead, the group paddled through most of them. Groups of Indians waited on both sides of the riverbanks, ready to steal from a tipped canoe. Luckily, the boats stayed afloat. Still, the rapids spooked Old Toby. When the men woke the next morning, the guide was gone. He had taken two horses as payment.

Eventually, the men noticed army jackets on some of the local Indians. They were getting closer to the sea. They saw Mount Hood, named by a sea captain traveling up the Columbia River. They were once again in mapped territory.

They were also entering Chinook territory. Twisted Hair turned back, since the Nez Perce were at war with the Chinook. Lewis and Clark met with the Chinook and continued west. On October 30, they camped at the cascades of the Columbia. Lewis and Clark called it the "Great Shute." It was the final drop-off before the tidewater began.

As they headed toward the ocean, the world around them changed. The desert became a rainforest, blossoming with life. Cedar, oak, and spruce trees loomed over them. Ducks and geese squawked noisily. On November 7, Clark believed he finally saw the ocean. "Ocian in view! O! the joy," he wrote. In truth, Clark saw the widening mouth of the Columbia. He would have a long time to get used to the sight. That night, a storm blew up. It kept the group pinned to their camp for three weeks. The waters were too rough to canoe on. Also, they couldn't walk along the steep rocky ledge. Eventually, the Corps was rescued by a group of Clatsop Indians, who were much better at paddling over the rough waters.

At long last, the expedition was within reach of the Pacific Ocean. Here, another important decision faced them. Where should they stay? Winter was coming quickly. They could camp on either the north side or the south side of the Columbia River. Lewis and Clark preferred the south side, which the Clatsop controlled. The Chinook controlled the north. A group of Chinook had tried to steal their rifles, and they didn't trust them. They could also camp further inland, which would put them in drier country.

Instead of making the decision themselves, Lewis and Clark put it to a vote. Each member of the party, including Sacagawea and York, cast his or her choice. Aside from John Shields, everyone voted to spend the winter on the south shore. Lewis and Clark had brought American democracy beyond America's borders.

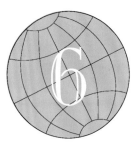

On September 23, 1806, Clark wrote in his journal, "Took an early breckfast . . . and set out, decended to the Mississippi and down that river to St. Louis at which place we arrived about 12 oClock." The Corps of Discovery had completed its mission successfully.

And Back Again

THE COMPANY established Fort Clatsop on the south shore of the Columbia River. As the Clatsop had told them, there were plenty of elk for hunting. Also, it was a good place to watch the coast. Life at the fort was mostly drudgery. Men boiled seawater to make salt. Everyone worked at repairing **leggings**, shirts, and moccasins.

The group ate roasted elk almost every day. Everyone was soon sick of it. Drouillard was the group's best hunter. On some days, he killed six elk on his own. That was a mixed blessing. On the one hand, the group wouldn't starve. On the other, they would survive to eat more elk.

In early January, Clark heard of a beached whale a few

miles down the coast. He gathered a group of men and went off in search of blubber. Sacagawea insisted on coming along. Lewis wrote, "She observed that she had traveled a long way with us to see the great waters, and that now that monstrous fish was also to be seen, she thought it very hard she could not be permitted to see either."

By the time they reached the whale, its blubber had been stripped away. It was simply a huge skeleton on the shore. Not wanting to return empty-handed, Clark traded for 300 pounds of blubber. Even that much couldn't feed them for long. Soon they were back to elk.

No ship ever came to Fort Clatsop. Jefferson's letter of credit had been useless. The entire expedition would have to trudge back to the United States by land. If they could not make it, all their work would be lost.

The group had hardly anything left to trade. Only a handful of trinkets remained. They had only their rifles, powder, scientific instruments, kettles, and journals. Lewis traded his uniform coat for a canoe. The night before they were to leave, they stole another canoe for the trip. This brought them to five canoes in all.

The next day, the canoe's owner confronted the company. Lewis offered him an elk skin for it, and the man took it, probably realizing he had no choice. He was facing 32 armed men desperate to get home. However, this was a serious violation of Lewis and Clark's ethics. The group broke a code of trust between themselves and the Indians.

It was difficult to paddle up the Columbia. The current was strong. Chinooks clustered around the men, hoping to steal something. One man was beaten for sneaking around the camp at night. When a saddle and a robe were stolen, Lewis threatened to burn down a village if he didn't get them back. Fortunately, he found the hidden goods before any houses were burned.

This was an extremely tense time for the men. The petty thefts of the Chinook didn't compare with the theft of a canoe. Lewis's temper, and perhaps his conscience, was getting the better of him.

In May, the group returned to Nez Perce territory, where they received bad news. The snows were still deep. The mountains wouldn't be passable until June. In the meantime, Lewis and Clark set up a hospital for the Nez Perce. In return, the Indians brought them dogs and roots. Some of the men traded buttons to get extra food.

The expedition started over the mountains on June 15. The Nez Perce thought this was too soon, but Lewis and Clark insisted. After two days, they found the snow was eight feet deep. Drouillard went back and offered a rifle for a guide who would take them over the mountains. This was the first rifle the expedition parted with.

York

York was born into slavery. From an early age, he was the slave and companion of William Clark. His father had served Clark's father all his life.

York was slightly younger than Clark. His life as a slave was probably unremarkable until Clark joined Lewis on the expedition. After the Corps of Discovery left St. Louis, York's life changed. He was treated like the rest of the company. York did his share of the camp chores, and attended to Clark on the journey.

The Native Americans that the party met had never seen a black man before. Clark writes in his journal about how the Indians would gather around York, amazed at his dark skin and curly black hair.

After the expedition returned home, Clark continued to treat York as a slave. York asked Clark for his freedom, or at least to be hired out to someone near where his wife lived, but Clark refused. It would be 10 more years before he finally freed York. Some believe York returned to the Mandan village where he had been treated as an equal. There is evidence that York opened a shipping company, moving freight from Nashville to Richmond. York died in Tennessee in 1832.

Three guides returned with Drouillard. The expedition crossed the mountains from June 23 to June 30. It took them six days to cover an area that had taken eleven days the year before.

Once across the mountains, the captains tried something daring. In hostile territory, still 2,000 miles from home, they split up. Clark traveled down the Yellowstone River. Lewis took the Nez Perce's trail to the Great Falls. The pair would reconnect where the Yellowstone fed into the Missouri.

Although Clark gathered a great deal of information on his trip, it was relatively uneventful. Lewis's party, on the other hand, was nearly killed. After splitting from Clark, Lewis split his party down yet again when they reached the Marias River. Lewis, Drouillard, and Reubin and Joseph Field headed north. The rest of the men stayed behind with Sergeant Ordway to prepare for the portage around the falls.

A few days later, Lewis encountered some teenaged Blackfeet Indians. He had been warned that the Blackfeet might try to take their supplies or weapons. They ate with the boys and smoked some tobacco.

That night, Lewis' group kept a tight guard. At one point, Reubin set his rifle down near his brother. One of the Blackfeet boys stepped out of the darkness and grabbed it. The Field brothers chased him, and Reubin wrestled him to the ground. He got his rifle back and then stabbed the boy through the heart. Another Indian was trying to steal Lewis's and Drouillard's guns. Lewis pulled his pistol, and the boy dropped the weapons. Just then, the other Indians

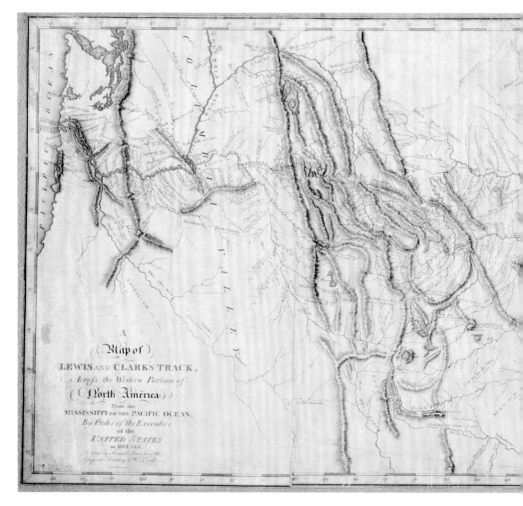

During their journey across the continent, Lewis and Clark took careful notes of the places they visited and the people they met. They also paid careful attention to their surroundings, keeping track of their latitude and longitude as well as the distances they traveled. This information would be used to create accurate maps

were setting their horses free. Lewis shouted for them to stop. One did, and turned on him with a musket. Lewis shot him in the belly. The wounded boy fired on Lewis, just missing his head. The boy and his friends ran off into the night.

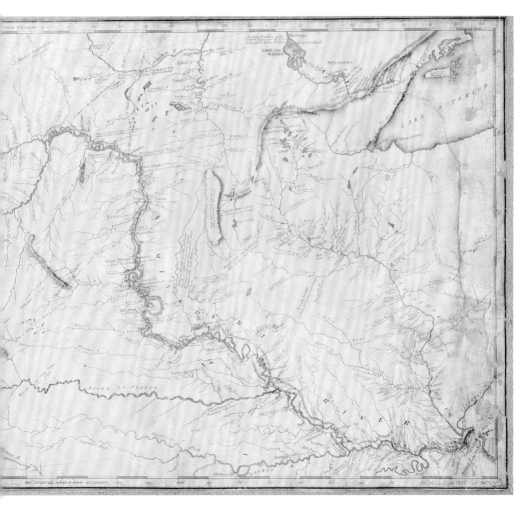

of the territory they explored. However, Clark did not publish the information in his journals, or make maps showing the party's discoveries, until 1814, when this map was made. Lewis never got around to editing his journals. They were not published until after his death in 1809.

The group had no time to spare. Soon, the entire Blackfeet nation could be after them. They gathered their horses, picked up their camp, and rode for 22 hours straight. At 2 A.M. the next day, they were exhausted. They had covered 100 miles.

The next day, they met up with Sergeant Ordway's crew. They soon were able to set their boats back on the Missouri once again. On August 12, they rejoined Captain Clark.

From there, the expedition made a brief stop at the Mandan village. There, they said goodbye to Sacagawea, Charbonneau, and their son. They paid Charbonneau $500. Sacagawea would later send Jean-Baptiste to Clark for his education.

On the way to St. Louis, they met with traders coming upriver. They bought tobacco and whiskey from them and received news of home. By the time they were in sight of St. Louis, word of their coming had preceded them. Thousands of people cheered them as they arrived.

Lewis wrote to President Jefferson immediately. He broke the news that there was no northwest passage. He gave Jefferson details of the trip, and praised Clark and the other men.

Lewis and Clark had a long, comfortable trip to Washington. Every city they stopped in threw them a party. In November, Lewis finally met with the president.

In this painting of Native American leaders, made in 1821 in St. Louis, the chief in the foreground is wearing one of the peace medals distributed by Lewis and Clark 15 years earlier.

Congress saw the value in the expedition, doubling the men's pay. Each received 320 acres for his service. Lewis and Clark were given 1,600 acres each.

The Corps of Discovery had crossed the continent. All but one member lived to tell about it. In payment, the government granted them land. More than anyone, they could see the value in their land. It was a small piece of a majestic continent.

Chronology

1770 William Clark is born on August 1; York is born.

1774 Meriwether Lewis is born on August 18.

1786 Sacagawea is born.

1794 Meriwether Lewis serves in the Pennsylvania militia during the Whiskey Rebellion; Clark takes part in the battle of Fallen Timbers.

1800 Sacagawea is kidnapped by Hidatsa.

1801 President Jefferson makes Meriwether Lewis his personal secretary.

1803 In April, Meriwether Lewis begins studying in Philadelphia to prepare for the expedition; Lewis offers co-command to William Clark in June; on July 4, President Jefferson purchases the Louisiana Territory from France for $15 million.

1804 On May 21, the Corps of Discovery leaves St. Louis; the Corps of Discovery encounters its first Indian tribes, the Missouri and the Otos, on August 2; on September 23, the Corps has a confrontation with the Lakota; on October 24, the expedition arrives at a Mandan village.

1805 On April 7, the Corps of Discovery leaves the Mandan village; from June 16 to July 14, the Corps portages around Great Falls; on August 12, Lewis reaches the source of the Missouri River; on August 17, Sacagawea recognizes her brother, Chief Cameahwait; the expedition crosses the Bitterroot Mountains from September 11 to 22; on October 6, the Corps of Discovery begins its journey down the Columbia River; on November 7, Clark spots the Columbian estuary; on November 24, the party votes on where to make winter camp.

1806   On March 23, the Corps of Discovery leaves Fort Clatsop; on July 3, the Corps temporarily splits into two parties; Lewis's group fights with and kills two Blackfeet teenagers on July 26; on August 12, Lewis and Clark reunite at Yellowstone junction; on September 23, Lewis and Clark arrive in St. Louis to cheering crowds.

1809   Meriwether Lewis commits suicide in Tennessee on October 11.

1812   Sacagawea is believed to die in South Dakota, although some historians believe she may have lived on in Wyoming until 1884.

1816   William Clark frees his slave York.

1832   York dies in Tennessee.

1838   William Clark dies in Virginia on September 1.

Glossary

ally—one that is associated with another as a helper.

bullboat—a circular Native American vessel consisting of a frame covered in buffalo hides.

celestial—relating to the sky or outer space.

chronometer—an instrument designed to keep time with great accuracy.

dead reckoning—a simple method of determining distances and positions by estimating distances from a known position.

dugout—a boat made by hollowing out a large log.

eddy—a whirlpool.

keelboat—a shallow, covered riverboat that is usually rowed, poled, or towed and that is used for freight.

latitude—the distance north to south.

leggings—a covering for the leg.

longitude—the distance east to west.

northwest passage—a sea passage believed to exist through North America that would connect the Atlantic Ocean to the Pacific Ocean.

portage—the carrying of boats or goods overland from one body of water to another or around an obstacle.

Glossary

snag—a tree or branch embedded in a lake or streambed creating a hazard to navigation.

toll—money paid to pass over a road or bridge.

trade relations—an agreement that allows trade between nations or groups of people.

unanimous—having the agreement or consent of all.

Further Reading

Ambrose, Stephen E., and Sam Abell. *Lewis and Clark: Voyage of Discovery.* Washington, D.C.: National Geographic Society, 1998.

DeVoto, Bernard, editor. *The Journals of Lewis and Clark.* Boston: Houghton Mifflin Company, 1981.

Duncan, Dayton, and Ken Burns. *Lewis and Clark: The Journey of the Corps of Discovery.* New York: Alfred A. Knopf, 1997.

Kozar, Richard. *Lewis and Clark: Explorers of the Louisiana Purchase.* Philadelphia: Chelsea House Publishers, 2000.

Marcovitz, Hal. *Sacagawea: Guide to the Lewis and Clark Expedition.* Philadelphia: Chelsea House Publishers, 2001.

Internet Resources

The journey of Lewis and Clark

http://www.lewisandclark-clark.org/

http://www.washingtonhistory.org/wshm/lewisandclark/index.htm

http://www.lewisandclarkeducationcenter.com/

http://www.pbs.org/lewisandclark/

http://www.nps.gov/lecl/

http://www.lewisclark.net/

http://lewisandclarktrail.com/

Publisher's Note: The websites listed on this page were active at the time of publication. The publisher is not responsible for websites that have changed their address or discontinued operation since the date of publication. The publisher reviews and updates the websites each time the book is reprinted.

Index

Photo Credits

About the Author

Rob Staeger lives and writes near Philadelphia. A former newspaper editor, he has written many short stories for young people and several plays for older ones. He has written several nonfiction books for Mason Crest Publishers, including *The Boom Towns* and *Games of the Native Americans*.